Arjun Singh

Temple Architecture and Iconography of Babour and Panjnara temples in Jammu Region

GRIN Publishing

Bibliographic information published by the German National Library:

The German National Library lists this publication in the National Bibliography; detailed bibliographic data are available on the Internet at http://dnb.dnb.de .

Imprint:

Copyright © 2014 GRIN Verlag GmbH
Print and binding: Books on Demand GmbH, Norderstedt Germany
ISBN: 978-3-656-86004-4

This book at GRIN:

http://www.grin.com/en/e-book/284488/temple-architecture-and-iconography-of-babour-and-panjnara-temples-in-jammu

GRIN - Your knowledge has value

Since its foundation in 1998, GRIN has specialized in publishing academic texts by students, college teachers and other academics as e-book and printed book. The website www.grin.com is an ideal platform for presenting term papers, final papers, scientific essays, dissertations and specialist books.

Visit us on the internet:

http://www.grin.com/

http://www.facebook.com/grincom

http://www.twitter.com/grin_com

Temple Architecture and Iconography of Babour and Panjnara temples in Jammu region-A probe

Dr. Arjun Singh.

Assistant Professor, Chanderprabhu Jain College of Higher Studies & School of Law, Narella. (Affiliated to Guru Govind Singh Indraprastha University, Delhi)

Introduction

In Jammu region *śikhara* temples both of ancient and recent origin are very common. These vary in regard to as they possess only the sanctuary or more parts of a typical *śikhara* temple. Some of the temple consist of a single cella in which the idol is housed and have an enter room or *maṇḍapa*. The ancient temples, however, are entered through an ornamented porch usually supported by two pillars. The early medieval temples in Jammu region are two types.

(i).   Firstly, *ṭriratha* embellished by a variety of carvings and architectural designs as in the case of temples at Krimachi and most probably the Devi shrine at Babour.

(ii).   The second type to be seen in all other temples at Babour, which are not *ṭriratha* in construction but are equally decorated with carved embellishments and architectural design.

The temple of recent origin do not possess such outer formalities except that they have large curvilinear *śikharas* with a small melon-type *amalaka* or simply a *bhumi* in some cases on the highest narrow point to serve as base for a metallic *kalaśa,* set of three *ghātās* diminishing upwards, topped by a lotus bud pointed upwards. The lower portion or *janghā* is invariably a rectangular construction, all constructed out of bricks, leaving no scope for carved embellishment, but only for architectural designs, embellishing niches, projections like eves, *bandhanas, ardha- śikharas* and the like.

Main features of ancient stone temples

These types of temples are entirely made of stone and are usually decorated with carvings, its conical spire or *śikhara* form that peculiarly is technically designed as the *śikhara* or a square cella, a small portico and a low platform. In the developed form a covered ambulatory or *pradakshinā* and a low tower is seen added to the original concept. In the centuries to follow more improvements and additions were made as a result of the gusto of building activities during the early middles ages and it attained a definite and well laid down concept and came to consist of the following structural design, *śaili.*

(a). The *vimāna* or the shrine

(b). The *antrāla* or vestibule

(c). The *maṇdapa* or the assembly hall

(a). The *vimāna* or the shrine

The *vimāna* is main structure, which contains inside the *garbhagṛiha* housing the idol of the deity to whom the temple is dedicated. The *vimāna* is surmounted by a high tapering tower called the *śikhara,* which in case of ancient structures is rendered somewhat circular in shape and curvilinear in case of temples of later centuries, both type being topped by an *amalaka* in some form crowned by a *kalasa* (finial), or only *amalaka* which is circular ribbed stone disk. The *garabhagṛihā* is dark, the only natural light it has is which enters it through its door from the *maṇdapa .*[1] A lamp is usually kept lighted, symbolic of the divine power illuminating the mysterious universe.

(b). The *antrāla* or vestibule

The *garbhagṛiha* is joined to the *maṇdapa through* the *antrāla* i.e. a small vestibule.

(c). The *maṇdapa* or the assembly hall

The *maṇdapa* is a pillared hall where the devotees gather to worship the deity. The outer door of the *maṇdapa* is sometime covered by a small verandah or porch called *ardha-maṇdapa, which* serves as the entrance portico and is in some cases open on all the three side, supported by two or four pillars in front. The *śikhara* type covered *pradakṣinā-path* or circumambulatory passage for going round the *garabhagrihā*, emanating from the left side of the *antrāla* and merging in it on the opposite side. This is to say the modified modern *śikhara* style, a result of the introduction of brick as the construction material.[2].

Approximately all around the city of Jammu there exist a number of ancient temples almost all of them are built in *śikhara*[3] style.

(1).   BABOUR GROUP OF TEMPLE, JAMMU

Babour, a small village is situated about 38 km. northeast of Jammu and nine km. north of Mansar lake. At this place there is a group of six stone temples of great antiquity.[4] The ancient name of the site is Babbapura referred twice in the *Rājatarangini.*[5] This ancient site is situated on a plateau, about 4.8 km. square in extent in Dansal dun of the inner hills. According to the tradition current among the people of the area there were thirteen temples but now only six exist in various stages of decay. There are reasons to believe that Babbapura was the capital of the *Duggar* from tenth century to the middle of fourteenth century. This period, Jammu had been forsaken as the seat of government due to recurring Arab and Turk invasions.[6] These temples suddenly came to light in the world of art and architecture in 1991 when world heritage week was dedicated to its temples which are constructed in unique style[7].

The largest of these six temples is situated to the east of the group. It is double structure with a pillared *maṇdapa,*(hall). The temple is built on a plinth 2.6 metre (8 feet) high. It is approached by a flight of steps from the west side. The plinth or *Jagati* is a square platform, about 16.50 meters each side. Its doorway which about 2.20 meters high and 1.15 meters wide, is profusely ornamented with carved human figures and floral reliefs. According to R.C. Kak, "the roof was supported on two rows of twenty four filled columns"[8]. The columns are surmounted by capitals. The chief distinguishing features of these capitals are extremely well carved with interesting large elephant heads and trunks. The roofs of monolithic columns are about 2.75 meters in height.

The *maṇdapa* has approach to two main sanctums each 2.15 meters square. These are intervened by a third sanctum. The two large sanctums have also a small *antarāla* each. The *antarāla* (porch) of all the three sanctums have twenty fluted columns surmounted by capitals. In addition to these sanctums there was a fourth one, smaller in size than others. Externally the whole of the stone construction was elaborately carved.

(i).   ANAND BABOUR SHRINE

There is a ruined temple situated away from the village on the raised bank of a *nala.* It is locally known as 'Anand Babour' temple. On a rectangular plinth, which is almost buried under ground, is a block of three chambers with a separate vestibule for each of them and the pillared hall or *mandapa,* in front of them. The entrance and some other parts of it are in such a ruined condition that it is much difficult to describe its architecture. Externally the temple is plain and sparsely decorated. The ornamentation includes human figures, animal's effigies, floral reliefs and images of deities. Almost all of these are in decay state.

This temple was also dedicated to lord Siva. A dancing Siva sculpture is preserved in the shed in Bhagwati temple. Its *amalka,* the broken set is kept nearby the outer wall of the temple.

(ii).   DEVI BHAGAWATI TEMPLE

From architecture point of view, the temple of Devi Bhagawati in the temple complex at Babour can be placed between 850 and 1050 A.D.[9] The shrine is a highly oriented structure built in stone. It comprises of a single chamber sanctuary with a *mandapa* in front. An entrance in its west wall enters the mandapa. The latter has flights of steps both inside and outside. The roof of the *mandapa is* supported on four round fluted columns, which stand on a plain base.

The temple walls were richly carved on the outside with divine figures and sacred motifs. These sculptured reliefs unfortunately are much mutilated. In the left jamb of the doorway is a figure of the river Goddess Ganga standing on crocodile. On opposite panel is another figure, completely obliterated and must have been of Yamuna. The lintel bore the *navagraha* in relief.

The temple courtyard is tormented with dressed and carved stones fallen from the temples. Two of these, almost as big as the one, which the figures of Ganga, bear images of Ganeśha and Bairava[10]. Figures of Vishnu, Lakshmi and Annapurna have also been discovered.

The inner sanctum contains two round shaped small *pindis* of brown colour emerging from the ground. Besides these, figures of Kali and Durga are also installed there. Kali is shown in standing posture, having four hands in which she is holding sword, *damru* and bowl respectively. A figure if lion is also depicted as standing behind her. The image is engraved on small stone slab black in colour. The figure of Durga is represented as riding a lion holding various weapons in her hands. This image is of white marble.

The most prominent are the images of Sun God and *Mahaveera*. There is a strange sculpture like that of a carved Naga kept in a niche chiseled out the main wall of the *Parikramā*. Other images include various incarnations of Śakti and Śiva. These temples are conspicuous of their *śikhra*[11] style. The whole temple complex is under the control of Archaeological Department. Worship in the Devi Bhagawati temple is performed by local priest.

(iii). BABOUR TEMPLE OR ŚHIVDIVĀLĀ

In the opinion of R.C. Kak, the temple situated in Babour proper and known to the people around as Śivadivālā is probably later in date than the other remains at this place. It had a *maṇḍapa* and *antarāla* or vestibule and the sanctum or *garbhagṛiha*. The *maṇḍapa* in front has altogether disappeared leaving behind only some traces of lower courses. The structure of the shrine which exists contains only the *garbhagṛiha* internally 2.20 meters and some 5.50 meters high ceiling in the form of concentric circles and an *antarāla* measuring 2.1x1.40 meter. The *śikhara* is in the shape of stepped pyramids with a narrow flat which is surmounted by an egg-like dome, on top of which is placed a ribbed *amalaka* which has on top *kumbha* (pitcher) or *kalsa* on which is planted a *triśul* and *dhwaja*[12].It seems that the super structure has been reconstructed out of some old material and new design. The shrine is living one and is visited daily by devotees from the nearby inhabitants. R.C. Kak observed that the temple was constructed over an older crumbled shrine, as some part of it i.e. the columns and *amalaka,* are very different from other parts. The relief work on the external surface of the wall is much later than the columns and some sculptures in the temple. The most outstanding is the Śiva-Pārvati group of black marble, including the Ganeśa and lance-bearing Kārttikeya and Nandi.

(iv). KĀLĀDHERĀ TEMPLE

Kālādherā or 'Black Shrine' is now in a ruined condition and any useful description of its architecture is very difficult. It stands on a large rectangular (*jagati*) plinth about 23.25 x 16 meters in dimension and about 3 meters in height, approached from the east by a flight of steps. The existing structure shows that the temple was much plainer than the other temples. Like other temples it has pillared hall which is at present roofless and a *cella* with an *antarāla* in their midst. The door jambs though chiseled finely are plain. The lintel above has a niche ornamented with floral designs. According to R.C. Kak, the capitals are similar to the columns of the larger temples and adorned with projecting *makara* heads facing the centre but have disappeared.

The bases of columns are plain, heavy and square. There are traces of pilasters also. The two free standing door jambs of the entrance to sanctum have each two niches with gees-arch carved on tops. Each of the niches contains a mutilated figure. The low remains of the wall show that the temple was externally well decorated with human figures, niches and floral motifs.

(v). ṬRIRATANA-TYPE TEMPLE

Near the Kālādherā temple, there is another ruined temple, which stands on a high platform (*jagti*), it contains three conventional portions marked out by the remains of walls i.e. the *cella*, preceded by an *antarāla* and the *maṇḍapa* the latter approached through the *mukhadvāra* on top of the flight of steps. The gateway is nicely decorated. Externally, the temple seems to be *ṭriratana* in style, with walls and offsets without much carved ornamentation. Only the outer surface of the structure of temple *cella* and *antarāla* is a little ornamented.

In addition to the main shrine, there are traces of two more shrines in the same compound; one is in front of the temple and other at the back of the temple to the right.

All the temples of Babour are built up of sandstone, which was available locally. The stone used for the construction of these temple seems to be little softer; hence were chiseled carefully and then employed. It is also noticeable that no mortar has been used in the construction of these temples. The stones used in the construction are not of a good quality stone, the builders used stone slabs of very huge sizes to ensure stability[13].

(2). TEMPLE AT PANJNARA

In Panjnara, a hamlet in the hills, a few miles distant from Rajouri, there are architectural remains of a magnificent temple locally known as the *Pāndu- Kund*. This temple is unique in the province of Jammu and rivals in grandeur the best preserved temples of the valley of Kashmir.[14] On stylistic grounds R.C. Kak assigns it to the 9th or 10th century A.D. The whole structure is in the form of a rectangle, with a peristyle (the term peristyle in classical architecture for a continuous colonnade surrounding a temple or court. The term is also applied to the inner court of a large house, surrounded on three sides by colonnades) and a central shrine. The gateway faces east. The peristyle consists of 53 cells and the gateway. Internally it measures 191 feet by 120 feet/58 meters by 36 meters. The superstructure of the central shrine has altogether crumbled down and the double basement, on which it stood, has been buried under the debris of the demolished superstructure.

The peristyle at Panjnara temple consists of 53 cells, each entered by trefoil arch surmounted by a steep pediment. The lintels of arches of this temple are supported on pairs of pillars with double capitals. The outer face of the gate is embellished with *kirṭimukhas* has miniature trefoil arches, alternating. Each cell measures 7 feet by 4 feet/2.15 meters by 1.20 meters entered by a trefoil entrance surmounted by a steep pediment on half engaged columns. However, the rows of cells have no corridor or colonnade in front of them. Nothing much can be said about the architecture of central shrine which is now a heap of debris.

The Punch-Rajouri tract was an integral part of kingdom of Kashmir since very early times. When Hieun Tsang visited Kashmir (631-633 C.A.D), he found all adjacent territories on the west and south down to the plains subject to the sway of the king of Kashmir, including more especially the smaller hill- states of *Rajapuri* and *Parnotsa* (Punch)[15]. Even Lohārkot (modern Lohrin) near Punch served at times the second capital of Kashmir and this town gave Kashmir the ruling Lohāra dynasty during the 11th century. During this period of long subordination to Kashmir the *Abhisāra* region received and assimilated influences from across the Rattan Pir and Pir-Panjal, especially in the field of sculpture and architecture.

REFERENCES

1. Charak S.D.S.& Billawaria Anita , *History and Culture of Himalayan States. Vol. VIII,* Jammu, 1997, p.34

2. *Ibid.,* pp.34-35.

3. Jerath Ashok, *Hindu Shrines of the Western Himalayas,* Jammu, 2001, p.9.

4. Billawaria Anita, *'Babour Temples of Jammu'* article published in Journal *Puratattva,* Bulletin of the *Indian Archaeological Society,* Number 33, Delhi, 2002-2003, p.146.

5. Kalhana, *Rajatarangini,* VII, p.538.

6. Hutchison & Vogel, *History of Punjab Hill States, Vol. II,* Delhi, 1994, p.342.

7. Jerath. Ashok, *op.cit,* p. 178.

8. Kak R.C., *Antiquities of Basholi and Ramnagar,* Delhi, 1972, p.21.

9. Billawaria Anita, *Babour Temples of Jammu, op.cit,* p.146.

10. *Ibid.*

11. *Ibid.,* p. 180.

12. Ganhar J.N., *Jammu Shrines and Pilgrimages,* Jammu, 1985, p. 151.

13. Billawaria Anita, *op. cit, p.* 148.

14. Kak R.C., *Antiquities of Bhimbar and Rajauri,* Delhi, 1973, p.14.

15 Stein M.A., Kalhana's *Rajatarangini,* Vol.I, London, 1900, p.87.